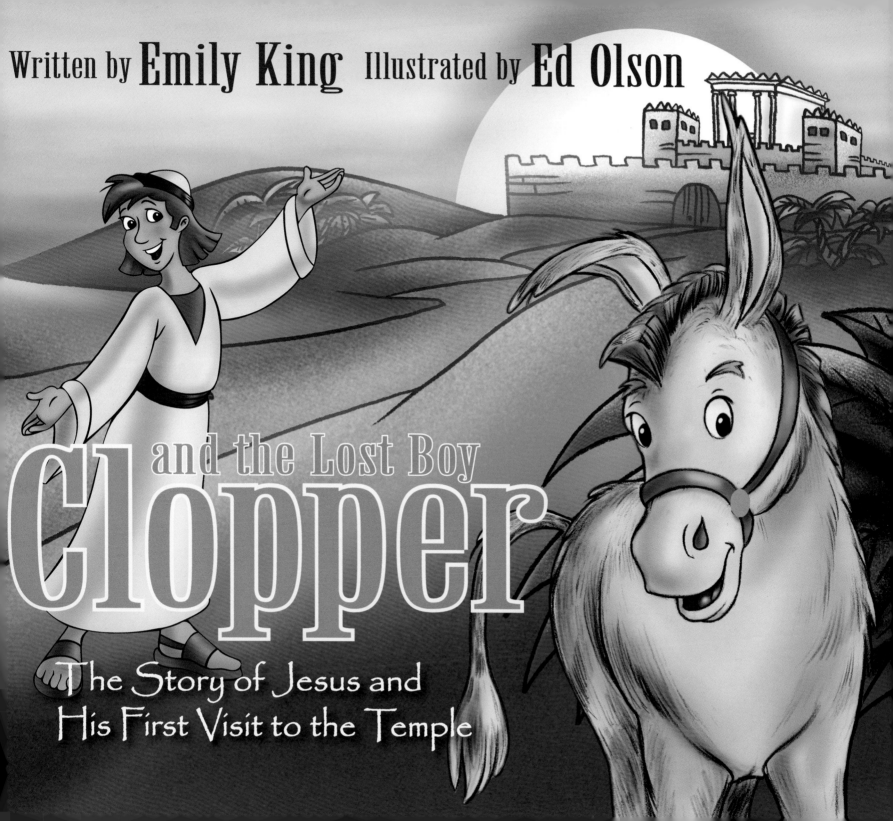

Written by **Emily King**   Illustrated by **Ed Olson**

Clopper and the Lost Boy

The Story of Jesus and His First Visit to the Temple

With love to
Drew, Jana, Caleb, Leslie,
Ryan, and Jamie.

"You will seek me and find me when you
seek me with all your heart." —Jeremiah 29:13

Clopper and the Lost Boy

Text © 2009 by Emily King
Art © 2009 by Ed Olson

Published by Kregel Publications, P.O. Box 2607, Grand Rapids, MI 49501.

Scripture quotations are found in Luke 2:40–52 and are taken from the *Holy Bible, New International Version*®. Copyright © 1973, 1978, 1984 by International Bible Society. Used by permission of Zondervan. All rights reserved.

ISBN 978-0-8254-2946-0

Printed in Hong Kong

My name is Clopper. Let's clip-clop down to the watering trough while I tell you about a very special celebration. One that caused quite a commotion!

The wildflowers were especially sweet that spring. I tasted some blossoms while Joseph and Jesus tied sacks of supplies on my back.

"I'm so excited," Jesus said. "Now that I am twelve, I can go to the Temple in Jerusalem to celebrate the Passover!"

And the child grew and became strong; he was filled with wisdom, and the grace of God was upon him.

Joseph nodded. "It's the most important of all the feasts."

"Yes," Jesus replied, "because Passover reminds us of the time God freed our people from bondage."

Jesus cinched up the last bundle, then scratched my ears. "There you go, Clopper," he said.
"Are all the supplies loaded?" Mary asked, closing the door behind her.
"Yes, Mother, we're ready to go!"

Hee-haw! Another adventure!

We joined the caravan of family members and neighbors on their way from Nazareth to Jerusalem for the celebration. I'd made the long trip with them many times before.

Every year his parents went to Jerusalem for the Feast of the Passover. When he was twelve years old, they went up to the Feast, according to the custom.

How wonderful this will be! A five-day journey of singing, music, and laughter.

Beneath a sprinkle of stars, families pitched their tents and warmed themselves beside flickering campfires as they talked and prayed.

Joseph and Jesus sang songs of praise to God and Mary smiled, humming along as she prepared the evening meal.

I munched hay and listened until my eyelids grew heavy and the music lulled me to sleep.

By the end of the fifth day, my hooves were beginning to ache. We rounded a hill and there it was—Jerusalem! The Temple glowed in the rosy sunset.

"There's the Temple!" Jesus said. "How beautiful are the courts of the Lord!"

The narrow streets bustled with travelers. I remembered our trip to Bethlehem years ago and wondered, *Will we all have to sleep in a stable again?*

Joseph knocked on the door of an inn.

"Yes, we have a room," the innkeeper said.

Jesus helped unload the bags, then fed me and gave me some water. He stroked my neck. "Tomorrow is Passover," he whispered. "I'll worship my Father and study His word at the Temple."

In the morning while Joseph, Mary, and Jesus went to worship, I snoozed in the courtyard of the inn. When they returned, we visited the marketplace to buy food for the Passover meal.

As we pushed through the crowd of shoppers, someone called, "Joseph! Over here!"

Standing beside a cart piled with tasty-looking fruit, a jolly round man waved at us.

"Samuel! My friend!" Joseph shouted. The men hugged and Mary said, "You remember our son, Jesus."

"Yes, of course," Samuel said. "I see you are growing up to be a fine young man."
The merchant chose a luscious apple and polished it on his sleeve. "For you," he said.
"Thank you, sir!" Jesus bit off a big, juicy chunk.
Samuel must have noticed me sniffing the fragrant fruit. "And one for you," he said.
I liked Samuel!

That evening, relatives came to share our Passover meal. I poked my head through a window and watched as Joseph said a prayer. Then, according to custom, Jesus recited the question a son was to ask on this occasion: "Why is this night different from all other nights?"

Joseph answered by reciting the Exodus story of how God delivered the Israelites from slavery in Egypt. The family sang a psalm, and then ate lamb and unleavened bread. They ended the meal with more songs and a prayer.

On the last morning of the celebration, Joseph, Mary, and Jesus went up to the Temple to worship. Afterward, family and friends gathered in the crowded Temple court, anxious to return to Nazareth. Finally, we set off on our long journey home. I clopped down narrow streets, listening to happy conversations and laughing children who ran ahead of the grown-ups.

After the Feast was over, while his parents were returning home, the boy Jesus stayed behind in Jerusalem, but they were unaware of it.

Joseph discussed the Scriptures with other men, while Mary enjoyed the company of her neighbors. Several hours passed, and Jerusalem had disappeared behind the hilltops.

"Joseph," Mary asked, "have you seen Jesus?"

"Not for a while," he answered. "But I'm sure he's fine. He must be up ahead with our relatives."

Mary frowned and glanced at the road behind us. "Yes. I . . . I'm sure you're right."

That evening, after each family had set up their tent and had built a fire for cooking, Jesus still hadn't returned.

"Don't worry, Mary. We'll find him," Joseph said. They darted from tent to tent, asking the same question: "Have you seen Jesus?" And everyone gave the same answer: No, they had not.

Thinking he was in their company, they traveled on for a day. Then they began looking for him among their relatives and friends.

Mary trembled and cried because she and Joseph could not find Jesus.

"We'll have to go back," Joseph said. "But it is too dark to travel now. It wouldn't be safe. We must wait until morning."

The hours crept by as we waited for sunrise. But no one slept that long night—inside or outside the tent.

When they did not find him, they went back to Jerusalem to look for him.

At dawn, we started back. It was late afternoon when we climbed the steep hills of Jerusalem. With the holidays over, normal life had returned to the city. People chatted, shopped, or scurried along.

Stopping people on the street, Joseph asked, "Have you seen a boy? Twelve years old? All alone?"

Mary's voice quivered as she questioned one merchant after another. They only shook their heads and went about their business.

When darkness fell, we returned to the inn. Mary softly wept, and Joseph comforted her. Through the night their prayers rose toward heaven and the heart of God: "Where is our son? Oh Lord, please watch over him and bring him back to us."

I hung my head and left my evening meal uneaten. I felt so lost and lonely without Jesus.

Again the next day, we wandered the streets of Jerusalem looking for Jesus.

"There's Samuel," Mary said. "Perhaps he has seen him."

When they asked, Samuel shook his head. "I am so sorry. I have no good word for you."

"My friend," Joseph said, "may we leave Clopper here while we search in the Temple?"

"Absolutely!" he answered. Mary and Joseph dashed away toward the Temple.

After a time, I heard Joseph shout, "Samuel! Praise the Lord!" I swung my head around to see . . .
JESUS! Hee-Haw! They had found Jesus!

"Thank God!" Samuel cried. "You have found him!"

"Yes!" Mary's face beamed as she hugged her son. "We saw Jesus sitting in the midst of the teachers in the outer court."

After three days they found him in the temple courts, sitting among the teachers, listening to them and asking them questions. Everyone who heard him was amazed at his understanding and his answers.

Jesus glowed with joy. "I have always sought the Lord and treasured His word with all my heart. So I was happy to join in the questions and discussions."

Joseph stroked his beard. With a look of wonder, he said, "All who heard were astonished at Jesus' answers and understanding."

When his parents saw him, they were astonished. His mother said to him, "Son, why have you treated us like this? Your father and I have been anxiously searching for you."
"Why were you searching for me?" he asked. "Didn't you know I had to be in my Father's house?"
But they did not understand what he was saying to them.

"So! You have been teaching the teachers!" Samuel laughed. "Here, lad! Have *two* apples!"
Then Mary spoke to Jesus. "We were so worried. Your father and I looked everywhere for you."
Jesus replied, "But Mother, didn't you know I had to be in my Father's house?"
Mary and Joseph glanced at each other with puzzled looks as if they didn't understand what Jesus meant.

"Let's go, Clopper!" Jesus said. We followed Joseph and Mary down from Jerusalem. After several days, we were back to our peaceful life in Nazareth.

I soaked up sunshine and perked my ears to hear the rapping and tapping of the carpentry shop as Joseph taught Jesus the builder's trade. Day after day Jesus grew stronger and wiser. Yet he always found time to scratch my head and slip me a tasty morsel.

Then he went down to Nazareth with them and was obedient to them. But his mother treasured all these things in her heart. And Jesus grew in wisdom and stature, and in favor with God and men.

I'll never forget the time we thought we had lost Jesus. And I'll always remember how happy I was to have him back.

I just couldn't imagine life without Jesus!